LIBRARIES

A TRUE BOOK

by
Lucia Raatma

Children's Press®
A Division of Grolier Publishing

New York London Hong Kong Sydney
Danbury, Connecticut

Reading Consultant
Linda Cornwell
Learning Resource Consultant
Indiana Department
of Education

Students at a college library

Visit Children's Press on the Internet at:
http://publishing.grolier.com

Library of Congress Cataloging-in-Publication Data

Raatma, Lucia.
   Libraries / by Lucia Raatma.
      p.   cm. — (A true book)
   Includes bibliographical references and index.
   Summary: Provides a brief look at the history of libraries, some differ-
ent types of libraries, and the services they provide.
   ISBN 0-516-20672-9 (lib.bdg.)   0-516-26380-3 (pbk.)
   1. Libraries—History—Juvenile literature. 2. Libraries—United States—
Juvenile literature.   [1. Libraries.] I. Title. II. Series.
Z721.R24 1998
027'.009—dc21
                                               97-18052
                                                   CIP
                                                     AC

Contents

A Home for Books

As you enter a library, you might be impressed by the number of books in it. You see books on travel and books about cooking. You see books about children and books about grown-ups. There are big books and small ones. There are serious books and funny books. How did all these books get in one place? Every book has a home in a library. And each book has its

Every book has its own special place in the library.

own special place. Libraries are organized so that you can find any kind of book you want.

Different libraries use different systems of organizing, but the two most common ones are the Dewey Decimal Classification and the Library of Congress system. Both use numbers and letters to keep track of books and where they belong.

For many years, people used a library's card catalog files to

find exactly where a book was located. Many libraries still use this system, but today, more and more libraries are putting this information on computers. You can ask your librarian more about how these systems work.

All Kinds of Libraries

When you think of a library, you probably imagine the library in your school or maybe the public library in your town. These are two kinds of libraries, but there are many other kinds.

Colleges and universities have their own libraries. These are used for research by the

students and professors at each school. There are also libraries used only by government officials. And there are special

A university library

libraries created for different professional people: bankers, engineers, lawyers, doctors, and scientists, among others.

Businessmen doing research at a business library

A doctor might use a library so she can study how other doctors have helped their patients. A lawyer might read legal cases to prepare for his own cases.

How Libraries Started

The history of libraries follows the history of writing. Ever since people have written down their ideas, they have collected their written materials in some way. Over the years, people recorded their ideas on a variety of materials: bone, clay, metal, wax, silk, leather, parchment—

13

and now, paper, film, and computer disks.

The first library was probably a collection of clay tablets in Mesopotamia. Mesopotamia was an ancient region that covered most of the present-day countries of Iraq, Syria, and Turkey. The Sumerians, who lived in Mesopotamia, made some of the oldest clay tablets five thousand years ago. In the ancient city of Nippur, scientists have found a library of thirty thousand such clay tablets.

The first library was probably a collection of clay tablets carved by the ancient Sumerians.

Writing Materials and Libraries

At the same time that the people of Mesopotamia wrote on clay, the people of Egypt used papyrus. Papyrus was a type of reed that grew in the Nile River. The reeds were cut into strips, pressed into sheets, and formed into long scrolls. The

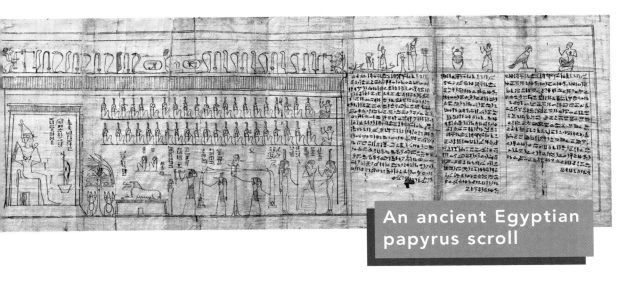

scrolls could be more than 100
feet (30.5 m) long.

Papyrus was not a strong
material and it fell apart easily.
Even so, some ancient writings
on papyrus still survive. Some
of these writings, displayed in
museums, date back to the
1100s B.C.

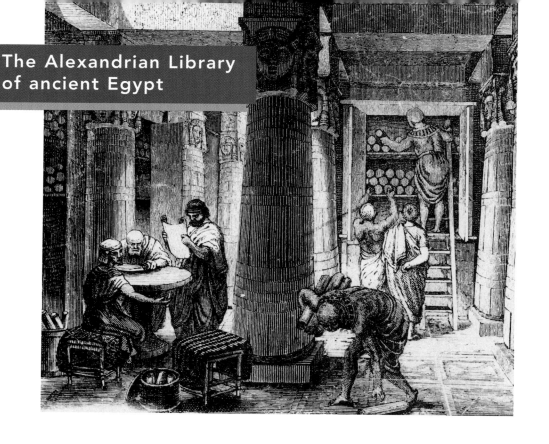

Egypt had one of the most
famous libraries of ancient
times, the Alexandrian Library.
This library was founded in
the 330s B.C. and held more
than 400,000 scrolls.

The people of Greece also used papyrus, and one of its cities, Athens, had a public library. Few people of that time could read, however, so only a small part of the community used the library.

Hadrian's Library, an ancient Greek library in Athens

Another writing material was parchment, which was made of thin layers of animal skin. Unlike papyrus, parchment did not roll easily into scrolls. Instead, parchment was folded and sewn like a book.

A German parchment book from the Middle Ages

A Christian monastery library founded in Austria during the Middle Ages

During the Middle Ages, people grew less interested in public libraries. During this time, Christian monasteries were very important in preserving libraries and encouraging education.

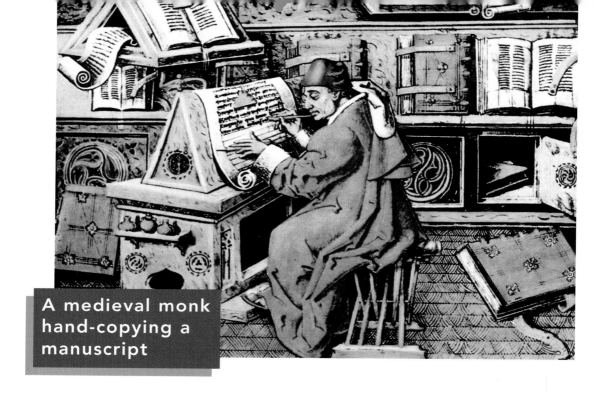

A medieval monk hand-copying a manuscript

Hundreds of years before the invention of the printing press, the copying of manuscripts was a popular activity in the monasteries. Monks would copy religious works, especially the Bible, and other works from ancient Greece and Rome. The monks sold some of the copies and kept others for their libraries.

A page from a manuscript hand-written and illustrated by a medieval monk

During the Renaissance

The Renaissance was a time of renewal for art and learning. Throughout Europe during the 1300s, scholars looked back to ancient writings and translated them. They also created new pieces of writing and works of art.

This era brought more interest in the creation of libraries, so

A library in Europe during the Renaissance

that new and old works could
be collected and shared.

In Rome, the Vatican Library
began in the 1400s. The library
serves the Roman Catholic

Church and keeps some very valuable literary treasures.

In England, the Oxford University library received a large collection of writings from the Duke of Gloucester in the 1400s. The library still has some of this collection today.

The Use of Paper

Although the Chinese invented paper as early as A.D. 1, it was not used for writing for about another 100 years.

Paper is made from wood pulp. As the making of paper spread throughout the world, people learned that it was the best material for

The Chinese invented paper about two thousand years ago.

writing. By the 1500s, it had replaced parchment as the most popular writing material.

As the interest in literature grew, scribes who hand-copied books could not keep up with the demand. The development of movable type solved this problem.

Separate metal letters were made. These were then set next to one another to form words on a wooden printing press. Ink was applied to the

The printing press allowed many more books to be made. More books meant more libraries!

surface of the letters, and then paper was applied to the press.

From Handwriting to Type

German inventor Johannes Gutenberg brought movable type and the printing press to Europe. The Chinese had used movable type for centuries.

Johannes Gutenberg (right) in his printing workshop

As movable type replaced handwriting, books were easier to produce. By 1600, library shelves began to fill with books and look something like they do today.

A library in Europe in the 1600s

Libraries Throughout the World

The British Museum was opened in 1759. It included a library as well as a museum. In 1973, it was renamed the British Library. It holds England's largest collection of books.

In Italy, many great libraries were begun. The Ambrosian

The British Library
in London, England

Library in Milan is known for
its collection of manuscripts
by scientists and monks. The
Laurentian Library in Florence
is famous for its medieval
collections.

The Bibliotheque Nationale began in Paris, France, as the royal library of King Charles V in the 1300s. Today it is one of the largest and most famous libraries in the world.

Libraries in the United States

In the 1700s, as the new nation was forming, most libraries in the United States belonged to ministers or to wealthy families. In 1731, Benjamin Franklin began the country's first subscription library. This meant that people could pay dues and become

Benjamin Franklin (left) began the first subscription library in the United States (below).

members of the library and then could borrow books for free.

One of the most famous private libraries belonged to Thomas Jefferson. When the Library of Congress burned in 1812,

Congress bought Jefferson's collection to use in the new library that was being built.

As the nation grew, more and more people looked to libraries for education and entertainment. Subscription libraries became more popular throughout the country.

Before long, people in the United States felt that public education should be free. Public libraries became free as well, as they are today. In Peterborough, New Hampshire, one of the first

Almost every city in the United States has its own public library (left). The New York Public Library in New York City has a huge reading room (above).

free libraries was founded in 1833. This idea spread, and soon, free libraries could be found all over the country.

Today, public taxes support public libraries so that libraries are available to all.

More than Just Books

Libraries are great places to find books. They also sponsor a number of activities. Libraries offer book clubs and career classes. They provide reference services, so users can call up special librarians for information. Sometimes libraries also have readings

by authors or offer story-reading afternoons for children.

In addition to books, libraries have collections of videotapes and audiotapes. They also have many different kinds of magazines and newspapers. Often, libraries have computers that can help you find books within the library or allow you to do research on the Internet.

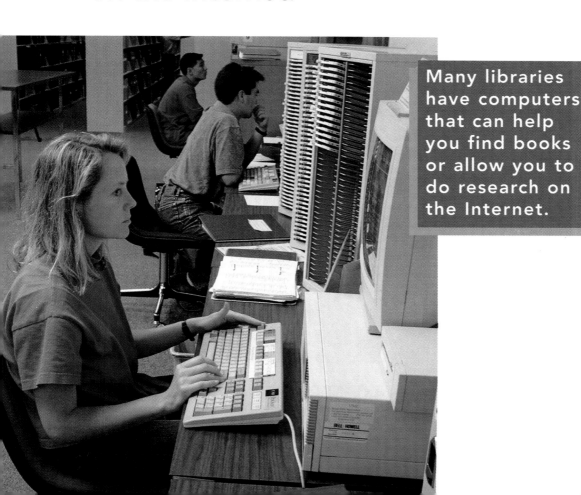

Many libraries have computers that can help you find books or allow you to do research on the Internet.

Today's libraries are bright and welcoming places. Some have open stacks. This means that anyone can browse through the shelves. Some libraries have closed stacks, which means you must ask the librarian for a certain book. But either way, libraries provide us all with a place to learn and to have fun. Whether you want to read about jewelry-making or cake-baking, skydiving or skyscrapers, South America or South Dakota,

Your local librarian can help you discover all the great things your library has to offer (left). A library can be a comfortable place to sit down with a good book (below).

your library will have a book for you. And your library will also have a librarian eager to help you find it.

To Find Out More

Here are some additional resources to help you learn more about libraries:

Books

Fowler, Allan. **The Dewey Decimal System.** Children's Press, 1996.

Fowler, Allan. **The Library of Congress.** Children's Press, 1996.

Knowlton, Jack. **Books and Libraries.** Harper Collins Children's Books, 1991.

Munro, Roxie. **The Inside-Outside Book of Libraries.** Dutton Children's Books, 1996.

44

Organizations and Online Sites

American Library Association

50 E. Huron Street
Chicago, IL 60611

ALA, the oldest and largest library association in the world, promotes the highest quality library and information services.

ALA Resources for Parents and Kids

http://www.ala.org/alsc/parents.links.html

Lots of library information sites, including lists of great kid's books to read and information on famous children's authors.

Internet Public Library

http://www.ipl.org/

Explore an online library that includes books to read and information to help with school projects. You can even ask a favorite author a question, listen to a story, or see what books other kids recommend.

Library of Congress

Jefferson Building
1st Street, SE
Washington, DC 20540
http://www.loc.gov/

The Library of Congress is the national library of the United States. It is the world's largest library and a great resource for scholars, researchers, and students. Its website presents information about materials from its collections.

The Whole Library Handbook

http://www. ala.org/alayou/publications/aleditions/wlh/wlh.html

Current data, advice, and information about libraries and library services.

Important Words

era period of time

literary having to do with written works

medieval having to to with the Middle Ages

Middle Ages the period in European history from about A.D. 500 to A.D. 1400

monastery place where monks live

monks men who have taken religious vows and live in communities together

Renaissance period in European history, from about 1400 to 1600, in which art, literature, and learning became very important

scholar person who does advanced study in a certain field

scribe copier of manuscripts

subscription when one receives a service— such as membership to a library—in return for a fee

Index

Meet the Author

Lucia Raatma spent many years in book publishing before becoming a free-lance writer. In the True Book series, she is also the author of *How Books Are Made*. She lives with her family in New York State.